I0813908

MOUNTAINS
Maria Koran
EYEDISCOVER

**Go to www.eyediscover.com and enter this book's unique code.**

**BOOK CODE**

**AVD44687**

**EYEDISCOVER** brings you optic readalongs that support active learning.

Published by AV² by Weigl
350 5th Avenue, 59th Floor New York, NY 10118
Website: www.eyediscover.com



Library of Congress Cataloging-in-Publication Data available on request

ISBN 978-1-7911-0758-1 (hardcover)

Printed in Guangzhou, China
1 2 3 4 5 6 7 8 9 0 23 22 21 20 19

072019
121818

Project Coordinator: John Willis
Designer: Mandy Christiansen and Sushant Deshpande

Weigl acknowledges Alamy, Shutterstock, and iStock as the primary image suppliers for this title.

EYEDISCOVER provides enriched content, optimized for tablet use, that supplements and complements this book. EYEDISCOVER books strive to create inspired learning and engage young minds in a total learning experience.

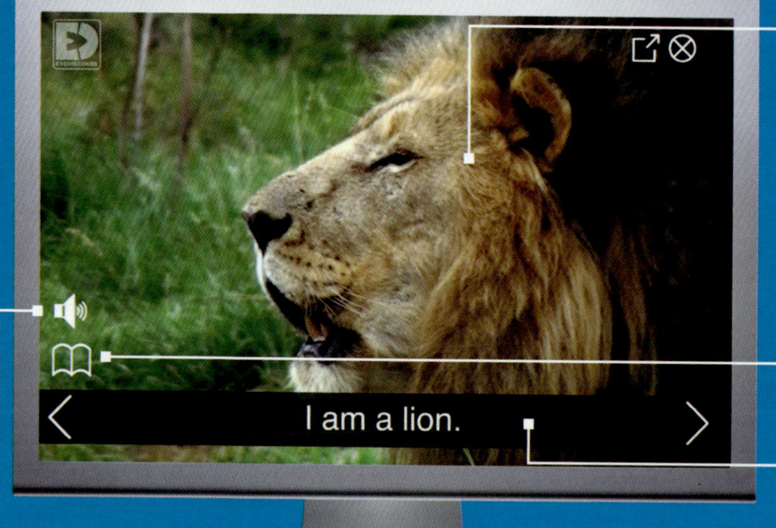


**Watch**
Video content brings each page to life.

**Browse**
Thumbnails make navigation simple.

**Read**
Follow along with text on the screen.

**Listen**
Hear each page read aloud.

## Your EYEDISCOVER Optic Readalongs come alive with...

**Audio**
Listen to the entire book read aloud.

**Video**
High resolution videos turn each spread into an optic readalong.

**OPTIMIZED FOR**

- TABLETS
- WHITEBOARDS
- COMPUTERS
- AND MUCH MORE!

In this book, you will learn about

- what they are
- what they look like
- where they are

and much more!

A mountain is a high area of land. A group of mountains is called a range.

The top of a mountain is called its summit or peak.

Some mountains are under the ocean. Underwater mountains are called seamounts.

Many mountains are covered in ice. Rivers can come from this ice when it melts.

Volcanoes make some mountains. The mountains form when lava cools and becomes rock.

People can do many fun things on mountains. In summer, people hike and climb.

In winter, many people ski and snowboard down mountains.

The tallest mountain in the world is Mount Everest. It is the highest point on the planet.

There are mountains on other planets, too. The tallest mountain in our solar system is Olympus Mons on Mars.

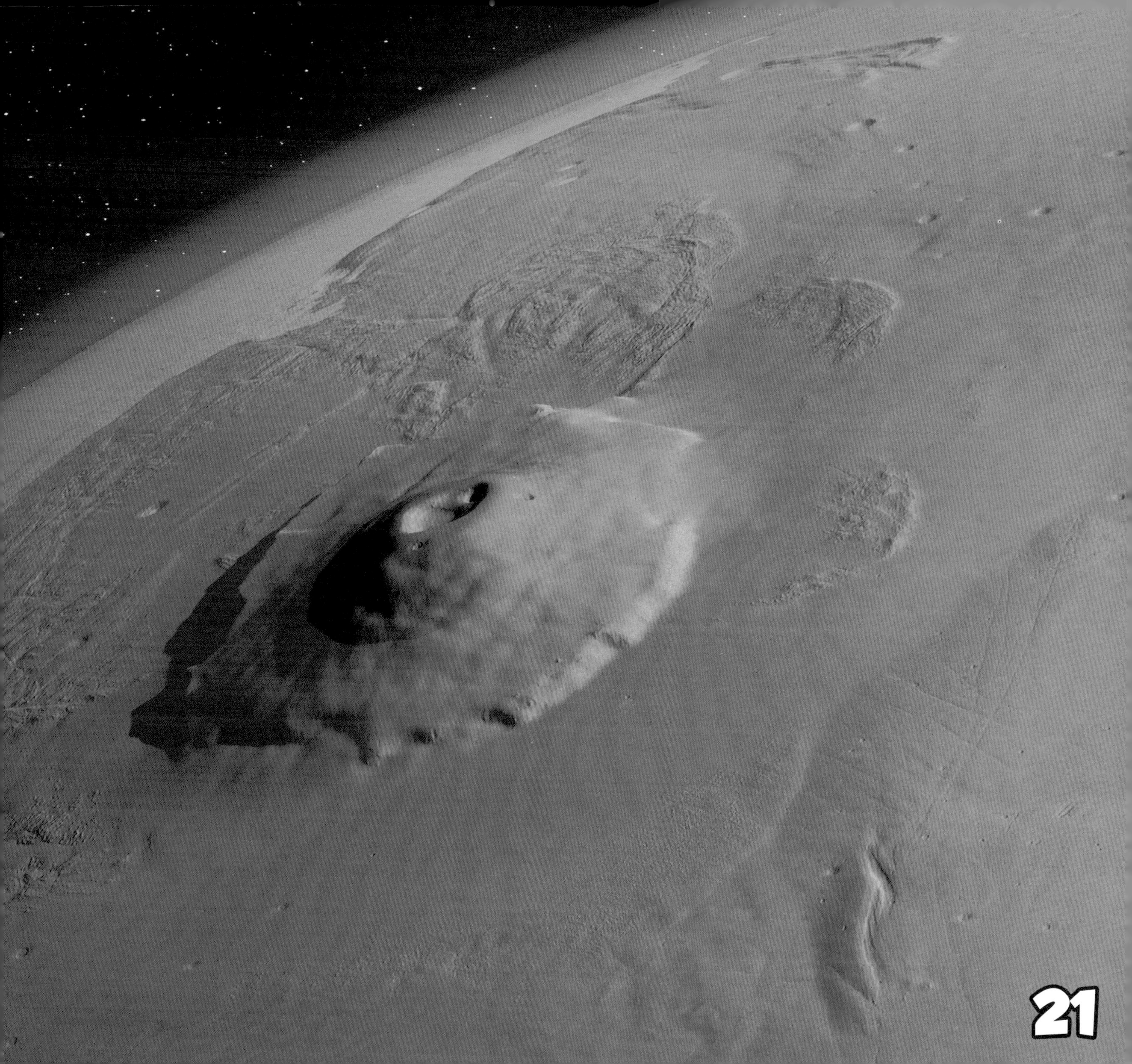

# MOUNTAIN FACTS

**Mountains** cover **one-fifth** of Earth's land surface.

A **mountain** is any landmass more than **1,000 feet** above the surrounding area. (305 meters)

More than **50 percent** of the world's fresh water comes from **mountains**.

**Mount Everest's** peak is **29,035 feet** above sea level. (8,850 m)

**Denali**, the highest mountain in the United States, is **20,310 feet** above sea level. (6,190 m)

**Olympus Mons** is **16 miles** high. (26 kilometers)

# KEY WORDS

Research has shown that as much as 65 percent of all written material published in English is made up of 300 words. These 300 words cannot be taught using pictures or learned by sounding them out. They must be recognized by sight. This book contains 34 common sight words to help young readers improve their reading fluency and comprehension. This book also teaches young readers several important content words, such as proper nouns. These words are paired with pictures to aid in learning and improve understanding.

| Page | Sight Words First Appearance |
|---|---|
| 4 | a, group, high, is, land, mountain, of |
| 7 | its, or, the |
| 8 | are, some, under |
| 11 | can, come, from, it, many, rivers, this, when |
| 12 | and, make |
| 15 | do, on, people, things |
| 16 | down |
| 19 | point, world |
| 20 | other, our, there, too |

| Page | Content Words First Appearance |
|---|---|
| 4 | range |
| 7 | peak, summit, top |
| 8 | ocean, seamounts |
| 11 | ice |
| 12 | lava, rock, volcanoes |
| 15 | climb, hike, summer |
| 16 | ski, snowboard, winter |
| 19 | Mount Everest, planet |
| 20 | Mars, Olympus Mons, solar system |

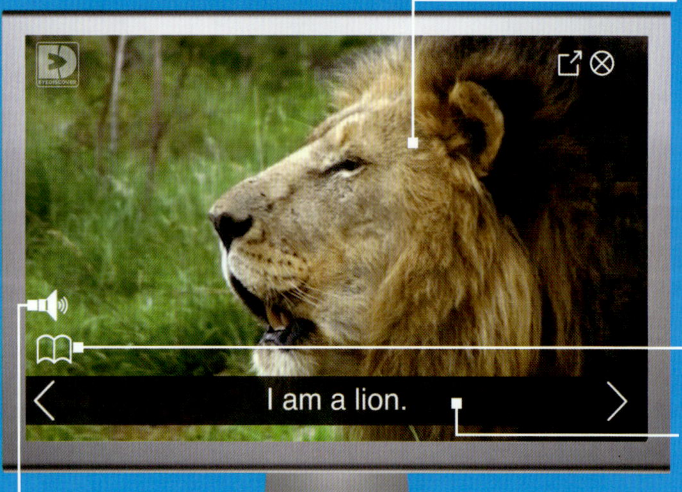


**Watch**
Video content brings each page to life.

**Browse**
Thumbnails make navigation simple.

**Read**
Follow along with text on the screen.

**Listen**
Hear each page read aloud.

Go to www.eyediscover.com and enter this book's unique code.

**BOOK CODE**

**AVD44687**